Unique Oregon

Margaret LaPlante

AMERICA THROUGH TIME®
ADDING COLOR TO AMERICAN HISTORY

America Through Time is an imprint of Fonthill Media LLC
www.through-time.com
office@through-time.com

Published by Arcadia Publishing by arrangement with Fonthill Media LLC
For all general information, please contact Arcadia Publishing:
Telephone: 843-853-2070
Fax: 843-853-0044
E-mail: sales@arcadiapublishing.com
For customer service and orders:
Toll-Free 1-888-313-2665

www.arcadiapublishing.com

First published 2022

ISBN 978-1-63499-412-5

Typeset in Mrs Eaves XL Serif Narrow
Printed and bound in England

Contents

About the Author

Margaret LaPlante is a historian living in southern Oregon. Her other titles for *America Through Time* include *Abandoned Jackson County: Towns Lost to Time*, *Abandoned Chinatowns: Northern California*, *A Unique Southern Oregon*, and *Oregon's Most Notorious Crimes: 1900-1955.*

Introduction

During the 1500s, ships from Europe and Great Britain sailed from the Atlantic Ocean to what Magellan named the Pacific Ocean, but no one had found a northern route. In 1543, Bartolome Ferrelo sailed from Mexico heading north in search of what was known at the time as the "Strait of Anian." Bartolome sailed part way up the coast before turning back, but never found the "Strait of Anian." In 1579, Sir Francis Drake sailed the *Golden Hind* part way up the coast and declared the land as "Nova Albion" in honor of Queen Elizabeth I. In 1601, Sebastian Vizcaino made it as far as 42-degree latitude before returning to Mexico. Years later, Martin Aguilar made an attempt to find a northern route up the coast before turning back. In 1774, Juan Perez, on an expedition for Spain, made it to the 54-degree mark. The following year, Bruno de Hezeta (AKA Heceta) came across a river with such strong currents he was unable to enter it. He named it Bahia de la Asuncion. Later, the name was changed to Heceta's Inlet. He was the first known man to come ashore and place a cross in Oregon soil, claiming it for the King of Spain. In 1788, Captain John Meares was sailing under the flags of both Portugal and Great Britain. He named Cape Lookout (known today as Cape Meares) and Quicksand Bay (known today as Tillamook Bay.) He did not enter what is now known as Cape Lookout. Captain Meares attempted to enter the same river that Bruno attempted, but was unable to. He changed the name from Heceta's Inlet to Deception Bay. Upon seeing the northwest coast, he wrote in his journal, "Wild in the extreme, immense forests covered the whole of it within our sight down to the very beach."

Upon learning of the challenge of finding the "Strait of Anian," Captain Cook made three attempts to discover this mysterious water. On his third and fateful last voyage, he did reach Yaquina Bay and Nootka Sound on Vancouver Island.

From there, he headed north but was killed before reaching his destination. The surviving members of his ship discovered that the sea otter skins they purchased from the Indians on the northwest shores were a valuable commodity in China. This created a fur trading business that grew competitive as more and more ships came along the coast.

When Major Robert Rogers of New Hampshire first learned of the country known by the Indians as "Ouragan" and "Origan," he decided it needed to be explored. He went to the King of England and requested funds to send a ship as far as "Ouragan." The funds were secured and Captain James Tute and Jonathan Carver set sail for parts unknown on September 12, 1776. It was after their voyage the name Oregon appeared on a map for the first time in Carver's Travels.

The following year, John Ledyard arrived in Boston and told of the great furs available on the other side of the continent. John had been with Captain Cook on his voyages along the west coast. A company was formed with the intent of sailing to the west and purchasing all the furs possible before heading to China to trade the furs for tea. Captain Robert Gray sailed the *Lady Washington* and Captain John Kendrick set out on the *Columbia Rediviva.* They encountered a storm and became separated, but Captain Gray was able to purchase some furs along the coast before heading to China.

Ships continued to come to the northwest shores and purchased, bartered and traded with the Indians for furs, beads, and commodities not available elsewhere. The years went by and then in May 1792, Captain Robert Gray returned to the west coast. He was at the helm of the ship the *Columbia Rediviva*. He manged to maneuver the ship up a stream of water near a large Indian village. Others had attempted to enter this stream of water, only to have to turn back. The stream had been named Cape Disappointment and Deception Bay for its seemingly impossible passage. Upon seeing a large ship approaching, the local Indians were astonished and immediately grabbed their canoes and rushed to the ship. Captain Gray traded the Indians copper items and cloth for a large quantity of furs before heading back up what he named the Columbia River. Later, Gray's Harbor was named for Captain Gray.

At the time of this discovery, George Vancouver was sailing in nearby Puget Sound. He had been unsuccessful in an earlier attempt to enter the Columbia River. After Captain Gray told him about the new river, he sent Lieutenant W. R. Broughton to attempt to enter the Columbia River. He made a successful attempt and was able to make it down the river. He is credited with naming the snow-capped mountain that overlooks the river: Mount Hood.

In July 1793, Sir Alexander MacKenzie, along with his crew, crossed the waters in Canada arriving at the Pacific Ocean at the mouth of the Bella Coola River. Upon learning of that feat, newspapers back east ran an article saying, "It would appear that shortly the northwest Pacific coast of this continent, now one of the least known in the entire world, will be laid open by daring explorers." In 1902, Sir MacKenzie wrote the book *Voyages from Montreal.* King George III of England awarded him the title of Knight Bachelor for his achievement in navigating the unchartered waters.

President Jefferson was becoming increasingly interested in what was west of the Mississippi River. The Louisiana Purchase had just been completed and he was intrigued by the possibilities out west. He had read books written by Sir MacKenzie and Captain Cook which only added to his urgency to find the best route to the Pacific Ocean. He met with John Ledyard and learned of the vast possibilities that lay on the other side of the country. Captain Gray's voyages had given America a foothold on the unexplored land and President Jefferson wanted to expand on that.

President Jefferson selected Meriwether Lewis to lead an expedition out west. Lewis, a native of Virginia, was thirty years old. He was a private secretary to President Jefferson. Later when President Jefferson was asked why he chose Lewis, he replied, "It was impossible to find a character who to a complete science in botany, natural history, mineralogy, astronomy, joined the firmness of constitution and character, prudence, habits adapted to the woods and a familiarity with the Indian manners and character, requisite for this undertaking. All the latter qualifications Captain Lewis has."

Lewis selected William Clark as his co-commander. Clark also hailed from Virginia. He was four years older than Lewis. Both men had served in the U.S. Army. Clark had been a Lieutenant of Infantry under President Washington before retiring from the U.S. Army. Four sergeants were selected for the expedition: John Ordway, Nathaniel Pryor, Charles Floyd, and Patrick Gass. Clark's slave, York, was selected for the journey. A few of the others selected included Joseph and Reubin Fields, George Drouillard, Joseph Whitehouse, George Shields, and John Colter. Additionally, there were many volunteers chosen for the expedition. Once the men were selected, President Jefferson explained, "The object of your mission is to explore the Missouri River, and such principle stream of it, as, by its course and communication with the waters of the Pacific Ocean, whether the Columbia, Oregon, Colorado or any other river may offer the most direct and practicable water communication across this continent for the purpose of commerce."

Congress appropriated $2,500 to defray the expenses "for the purpose of extending the external commerce of the United States." The government also gave approved lines of credit and put the members on the U.S. Army's payroll. They were tasked with crossing the Continental Divide to reach the Pacific Ocean.

The preparations for the expedition took an entire year. They ordered a keel-boat to be built by a carpenter who lived near Pittsburg. They laid in a supply of weapons and ammunition for hunting. Some of the other items they acquired included medical supplies, extra clothing, oilcloth, tools, compasses, quadrants, plotting instruments, a Chronometer, maps, books, binoculars, hatchets, chisels, handsaws, oilskin bags, blankets, materials for constructing tents, writing materials to document their experience, and fishing equipment. Some of the food items they packed included 1,000 pounds of corn, thirty half-barrels of flour, seven barrels of salt, fifty kegs of pork, 100 pounds of beans and peas, 112 pounds of sugar, one keg of hog's lard, soap and candles, steels for making fires, and extra clothing and shoes.

Additionally, they took many items to present as gifts to the Indians that they encountered along the way. Among the gifts were knives, beads, face paint, flags, thread, tobacco, small scissors, sewing supplies, cloth, and binoculars. President Jefferson asked the U.S. Mint to create silver medals to present to Indian Chiefs as peace tokens. The front of each medal was stamped with a likeness of President Jefferson. On the back of each medal was a pipe and a tomahawk crossed over a pair of hands. Written below were the words "Peace and Friendship."

The President tasked the members of the expedition with taking notes of the flora, fauna, animals, and the inhabitants they encountered along the way. During the year of preparation, Lewis and Clark brushed up on the skills they would need to make this a successful expedition. They studied medicine, astronomy, plant, and animal species. They practiced working with compasses and navigation tools. Additionally, Lewis spent time at Monticello studying the books and maps that President Jefferson had in his library.

Finally, the day came and the Corps of Discovery Expedition began. On May 14, 1804, Clark and his team set out in the keelboat and two pirogues. Clark wrote in his journal:

> Monday 14th a cloudy morning, fixing for a start. Some provisions on examination is found to be wet. Rain at 9 o'clock. Many of the neighbours came from the countrey mail and freemail. Rained the greater part of the day. Set out from Camp River a Dubois at 4 o'clock P.M. and proceeded up the Missouris under Sail to the first Island in the Missouri and Camped the upper point opposit a Creek on the South Side below a ledge of limestone rock Called Colewater, made 4 ½ miles. The Party Consisted of two, Self, one Frenchman and twenty-two men in the Boat of twenty ores, 1 Serjt and 7 French in a large Perogue, a Corp and six Soldiers in a large Perogue. A Cloudy rainey day, wind from the N.E. Men in high Spirits. Rained the forepart of the day. I determined to go as far as St. Charles, a French Village 7 leags up the Missourie,

> and wait at that place until Captain Lewis Could finish the business in which he was obliged to attend to at St. Louis and join me by Land from that place 24 miles, by this movement I calculated that if any alterations in the loading of the Vestles or other Changes necessary, that they might be made at St. Charles.

Upon embarking on the adventure, Patrick Gass wrote in his journal:

> On Monday the 14th of May 1804, we left our establishment at the mouth of the river du Bois or Wood River, a small river which falls into the Mississippi, on the east-side, a mile below the Missouri, and having crossed the Mississippi proceeded up the Missouri on our intended voyage of discovery, under the command of Captain Clarke. Captain Lewis was to join us in two or three days on our passage.

Joseph Whitehouse wrote about this important day:

> Monday, 14th May 1804. Hard Showers of rain this being the day appointed by Captain Clark to set out, a number of the sitizens of Gotain Settlement came to see us start. We got in readiness. Captain Lewis is now at St. Louis but will join us at St. Charles. About 3 o'clock P.M. Captain William Clark and the party consisting of three Sergeants and thirty-eight men who manned the Batteaux and perogues. We fired our Swivel on the bow hoisted sail and Set out in high Spirits for the western Expedition. We entered the mouth of the Missourie haveing a fair wind Sailed about six miles and Camped on the North Side.

Men on horseback followed the river so that the group would have access to the horses when needed. They headed to St. Charles, Missouri, to pick up Lewis. When they arrived at St. Charles, Joseph Whitehorse wrote:

> We set out this morning, having clear weather and proceeded on very well. About 2 o'clock P.M. we arrived at Saint Charles where we passed the Evening with a great deal of satisfaction, and chearfulness, and all our men appeared to be in good spirits. Saint Charles is a Village settled by French Inhabitants. It is a handsome situation, laying on the North side of the River contains about 80 Houses, built in the French fashion, and has a small Roman Catholic chapel. Its Inhabitants are chiefly Canadian French, who are chiefly concerned and employed by others Trading with the Indians who reside on the River Mesouri, and other Rivers that empty into it. The land adjourning it appear to be hilly, but the soil is good and fitting for Agriculture.

Patrick Gass wrote about leaving St. Charles:

> We remained at St. Charles until the 21st, where Captain Lewis arrived from St. Louis and joined us. At 4 o'clock in the afternoon we left this place under a salute of three cheers from the inhabitants, which we returned with three more and a discharge of three guns. This evening was showery, and we again encamped on the north side of the river.

One of the things that President Jefferson emphasized was to not only observe the Indians and their culture, but to represent the government and become allies with them. Clark wrote about meeting the Mandan Indians:

> A fine morning, the Chief of the Mandans Sent a 2d Chief to invite us to his Lodge to receive Some Corn and here[hear] what he had to Say. I walked down and with great ceremoney was Seeted on a roab by the side of the Chief, he threw a handsom Roabe over me and after smoking the pipe with Several old men around, the Chief Spoke. Said he believed what we had told them, and that peace would be general, which not only gave him Satisfaction but all his people, they Could now hunt without fear and their womin Could work in the fields without looking every moment for the Enemey, and put off their mockersons at night.

Joseph Whitehouse described the Mandan Indian's village:

> The Men that went with Captain Clark found among the Indians at this Village, Corn, Beans, Simlins, and many kind of Garden Vegetables. They and the Rick a Ree nation are the only Indians that we saw that cultivated the Earth, that reside on the Mesouri River. Their Village consisted of about 200 Lodges built in the manner, that the Rick a Ree build their lodges. This Village we supposed contained 1500 Souls. They were governed by a Chief called the Black Cat. They behaved extremely kind to the party, and the only animal that was among them, was some horses, which are stout serviceable Animals. This Village was situated on a large high plain, and they plant in the Bottom lying below it and to appearance are a very Industrious set of people.

The expedition team began in the middle of May 1804. By the middle of October, the weather was making their progress exceedingly difficult. It became obvious they would need to settle somewhere for the winter. At the beginning of November 1804, they began building what became known as Fort Mandan. It was located in McLean County, North Dakota, fourteen miles west of Washburn.

On November 4, 1804, John Ordway described building their winter home:

> Cold last night and white frost this morning, clear and pleasant. We continued raiseing our huts. Several more of our French hands is discharged and one making a pearogue in order to descend the Missourie. And Several of the natives come to our Camp to See us build our huts, and to See our boats. We got one line of our huts raised so that we got the Eve Beames on and all of the large Timber So that it took all of the men hard lifting to put the 16 foot eve Beames.

Once settled in to their first winter homes, John Ordway described trading with the Mandans Indians:

> Clear and cold this morning. A great number of Mandans came to Trade with us. They Bought us corn and Beans, Squasshes, also Some kind of Bread which they make of pearched corn and beans mixed together in round balls.

While spending the winter at Fort Mandan, the expedition team met Toussaint Charbonneau and one of his wives, Sacagawea, who was pregnant with her first child. Charbonneau was hired by Lewis and Clark to accompany the expedition team and assist with translating with the Indians. On February 11, 1805, while the team was encamped at Fort Mandan, Sacagawea gave birth to a baby boy. She named the child Jean Baptiste. Lewis wrote in his journal about the birth, saying:

> The party that were ordered last evening set out early this morning, the weather was fair and cold wind N.W. about five oclock this evening one of the wives of Charbono [Charbonneau] was delivered of a fine boy. It is worthy of remark that this was the first child which this woman had boarn and it is common in such cases her labour was tedious and the pain violent; Mr. Jessome informed me that he had freequently administered a small portion of the rattle of the rattle-snake, which he assured me had never failed to produce the desired effect, that of hastening the birth of the child; having the rattle of a snake by me I gave it to him and he administered two rings of it to the woman broken in small pieces with the fingers and added to a small quantity of water. Whether this medicine was truly the cause or not I shall not undertake to determine, but I was informed that she had not taken it more than ten minutes before she brought forth. Perhaps this remedy may be worthy of future experiments, but I must confess that I want faith as to its efficacy.

During the winter, new boats were constructed, and more supplies were acquired. On April 7, 1805, the team placed the new boats in the water and resumed their journey. In addition to Charbonneau, Sacagawea and Jean Baptiste, one of the Mandan Indians requested to travel with the team in the hopes of meeting with the Shoshone Indians to further peace talks between the tribes.

Although the worst of the weather was behind them, they still encountered frost and ice. They experienced water freezing on their oars, ice on their kettles, and severe wind storms on the water. Undeterred, they described the scenery, "country beautiful in the extreme."

Food could be scarce along the way. In some parts there was good hunting and fishing, but in other parts there were few opportunities to replenish their supply. Clark wrote about the need for additional food by saying, "The weather still continues cold cloudy and rainy, the wind also has blown all day with more than usual violence from the N.W. This morning we eat the last of our birds and cows, I therefore directed Drewyer and J. Fields to take a couple of the horses and proceed S.E. as far as the main branch of Maria's river which I expected was no great distance and indeavour to kill some meat." He later wrote that he had killed nine pigeons that they consumed. Another time Clark wrote, "We set out at sunrise and proceeded on very well for three hours. Saw a large gange of Buffalow on the land bark. I concluded to halt and kill a fat one, during which time some brackfast was ordered to be cooked. We killed 2 Buffalow and took as much of their flesh as I wished. Shields killed two fat deer and after a delay of one hour and a half we proceeded on."

At President Jefferson's request, the team studied the flora and fauna they encountered on their journey. When they were near Yellowstone, Clark wrote about wood willows, rose bushes, red goose berries, wild cherry, cottonwood trees, ash trees, and elm trees.

The team arrived at what they called "The Gates of the Rocky Mountains." Clark described the sight: "This evening we entered much the most remarkable clifts that we have yet seen." Seeing the Rocky Mountains for the first time, Lewis wrote:

> In the after part of the day I also walked out and ascended the river hills which I found sufficiently fortiegueing. On arriving to the summit one of the highest points in the neighbourhood I thought myself well repaid for any labour, as from this point I beheld the Rocky Mountains for the first time, I could only discover a few of the elivated points above the horizon, the most remarkable of which by my pocket compass I found bore 65° W. being a little to the N. of the N.W. extremity of the range of broken mountains seen this morning by Captain C. These points of the Rocky Mountains were covered with snow and the sun shone on it in such a manner as to give me the most plain and satisfactory view. While I viewed these mountains I felt a secret pleasure in finding myself so near the head of the heretofore conceived boundless

> Missouri; but when I reflected on the difficulties which this snowey barrier would most probably throw in my way to the Pacific, and the sufferings and hardships of myself and party in them, it in some measure counterballanced the joy I had felt in the first moments in which I gazed on them; but as I have always held it a crime to anticipate evils I will believe it a good comfortable road until I am compelled to believe differently.

Later the expedition team described seeing the plains. Whitehouse wrote, "We passed along Smooth plains, covered with high Grass and wild hyssop but the soil poor. There was no Timber to be seen here excepting some pitch pine trees." Gass described the plains, "We have now got into a country which presents little to our view, but scenes of barreness and desolation, and see no encouraging prospects that it will terminate."

"Ocean in view! O the joy!" wrote Clark on November 7, 1805. The purpose of their expedition was coming to a successful conclusion.

On November 16, 1805, Joseph Whitehouse wrote:

> We are now in plain view of the Pacific Ocean. The waves rolling, and the surf roaring very loud. On the opposite shore to us we discovered, the Tops of trees which we supposed to be an island laying a very great distance in the Ocean. We are now of opinion that we cannot go any further with out Canoes, and think that we are at an end of our Voyage to the Pacific Ocean, and as soon as discoveries necessary are made, that we shall return a short distance up the River and provide our Selves with Winter Quarters, and We suppose that we shall find a considerable Quantity of Game low down on the River.

Patrick Gass wrote about this momentous occasion saying:

> This was a clear morning and the wind pretty high. We could see the waves, like small mountains, rolling out in the ocean, and pretty bad in the bay. We are now at the end of our voyage, which has been accomplished according to the intention of the expedition, the object of which was to discover a passage by the way of the Missouri and Columbia rivers to the Pacific Ocean; notwithstanding the difficulties, privations and dangers, which we had to encounter, endure, and surmount.

As they approached the end of their journey, they began to experience harsh weather as winter was fast approaching. On November 28, 1805, Clark described their hardships:

Wind Shifted about to the S.W. and blew hard accompanied with hard rain all last night, we are all wet, bedding and Stores, haveing nothing to keep Selves or Stores dry, our Lodge nearly worn out, and the pieces of Sales and tents So full of holes and rotten that they will not keep any thing dry, we Sent out the most of the men to drive for deer, they Scattered through the point, some Stood on the pensolu, we Could find no deer. Several hunters attempts to penetrate the thick woods to the main South Side without Suckess, the Swan and gees wild and cannot be approached, and wind to high to go either back or forward, and we have nothing to eate but a little Pounded fish which we purchasd at the Great falls. This is our present Situation, truly disagreeable. Aded to this the robes of our Selves and men are all rotten from being Continually wet, and we Cannot precure others, or blankets in their places.

When it was time to decide where the expedition members would winter, each member was allowed to vote, including Sacagawea and Clark's slave, York. On Sunday, November 24, 1805, John Ordway wrote:

A clear pleasant morning. A white frost. Several men went out hunting. We put out our baggage to air. The Columbia River at this place is three miles 660 yards wide. Some of two nations of Indians came to our Encampment the Clatsop and Chinuck nations they behave very well as yet. Our officers conclude with the oppinion of the party to cross the River and look out a place for winter quarters. Some where as near the ocean as possible on the account of makeing salt.

On December 12, 1805, Clark wrote:

Some moderate showers last night and this morning. All hands are well employed in building cabins, detached two men to split boards. The flees so troublesome last night that I made but a broken nights rest, we find great dificuelty in getting those trouble insects out of our robes and blankets. In the evening two canoes of Clat Sops Visit us, they brought with them Wap pa to, a black sweet root they call Sha-na-toe-qua and a Small Otter Skin, all of which we purchased for a few fishing hooks and a small sack of Indian tobacco which was given by the Snake Indians.

On Christmas Day 1805, Patrick Gass wrote:

Was another cloudy wet day. This morning we left camp and moved into our huts. At daybreak all the men paraded and fired a round of small arms, wishing the Commanding Officers a merry Christmas. In the course of the day Capt. Lewis and

> Capt. Clark collected what tobacco remained, and divided it amongst those who used tobacco, as Christmas-gift, to the others they gave handkerchiefs in lieu of it. We had no spiritous liquors to elevate our spirits this Christmas, but of this we had but little need, as we were all in very good health. Our living is not very good; meat is in plenty, but of an ordinary quality, as the elk are poor in this part of the country. We have no kind of provisions but meat, and we are without salt to season that.

On New Year's Day 1806, Joseph Whitehouse wrote:

> At day break, the Men of the fort fired several Guns, as a salute to our Commanding officers, and in honor of the day. The Morning was pleasant. Two of our party were sent out to hunt. Several Indians came to the fort on a visit.

The expedition team got along well with the Indians during their stay at Fort Clatsop. There were frequent visits between the two parties. Joseph Whitehouse wrote:

> We had a pleasant morning but cool, the men that were Sick in the Fort, were all getting better. Several Indians of the Clatsop Nation came to the fort in Canoes. They brought with them Split and Straw hatts for sale. they make those kind of hatts by platting them very ingeniously and they were truly handsome. Towards Evening they left the fort, and one of our Hunters accompanied them.

The weather proved difficult with the men writing about fierce storms. Clark described having great difficulty digging one of the boats out of the ice. They frequently wrote about heavy rain and hail storms with tremendous winds. Regardless of the storms, they still had to go out and hunt in order to have enough food for everyone. There were cases of frost bite suffered while out hunting. But as the weather improved, it was time to prepare to leave Fort Clatsop and return home.

On March 23, 1806, Clark described their time in Oregon, writing:

> We loaded our canoes and at 1 p.m. left Fort Clatsop on our homeward bound journey. At this place we had wintered and remained from 7th of December 1805 to this day and have lived as well as we had any right to expect, and we can Say that we were never one day without 3 meals of Some kind a day, either pore Elk meat or roots, notwithstanding the repeated falls of rain which has fallen almost constantly.

In summing up their time in Oregon, Lewis wrote:

> Altho' we have not fared sumptuously this winter and spring at Fort Clatsop, we have lived quite as comfortably as we had any reason to expect we should; and have accomplished every object which induced our remaining at this place except that of meeting with the traders who visit the entrance of this river. Our salt will be very sufficient to last us to the Missouri where we have a stock in store. It would have been very fortunate for us had some of those traders arrived previous to our departure from hence, as we should then have had it in our power to obtain an addition to our stock of merchandize, which would have made our homeward bound journey much more comfortable.

Prior to leaving, they wrote a note and posted it in the fort. They wrote copies of the note and gave them to the Indian Chiefs, asking that they in turn give the note to any ships that arrived. The note said:

> The object of this last is that through the medium of some civilized person who may see the same, it may be known to the world, that the party consisting of the names hereunto annexed, and who were sent by the government of the United States to explore the interior of the Continent of North America, did penetrate the same by the way of the Missouri and Columbia rivers, to the discharge of the latter into the Pacific Ocean, where they arrived on the 14th day of November, 1805, and departed the 23rd day of March 1806, on their return to the United States, by the same route by which they had come out.

The return expedition proved difficult with the weather and hunting playing key roles. Clark wrote:

> Sent out Hunters this morning. Colter killed a deer and brought it in by 10 A.M. Drewyer did not return until night, he wounded deer but could not get none, neither of the other hunters killed nothing. We had our articles packed ready for a Start in the morning, our horses Collected and hobble that they may not detain us in the morning. we expect to Set out early, and shall proceed with as much expedition as possible over those Snowey tremendious mountains which has detained us near five weeks in this neighbourhood waiting for the Snows to melt Sufficient for us to pass over them. And even now I Shudder with the expectation with great dificuelties in passing those Mountains, from the debth of Snow and the want of grass Sufficient to Subsist our horses as about 4 days we shall be on the top of the Mountain which we have every reason to believe is Covered with Snow the greater part of the year.

The team made it over the mountains and although they were still plagued with bad weather and the fear of running out of food, they managed to do exactly what they had set out to do eighteen months prior. They had crossed the Continental Divide and found a route to the Pacific Ocean. On September 23, 1806, they returned to St. Louis. John Ordway wrote, "We delayed a Short time and about 12 oClock we arrived in Site of St. Louis, fired three rounds as we approached the Town and landed oppocit the center of the Town, the people gathered on the Shore and Huzzared three cheers." Clark wrote, "We Suffered the party to fire off their pieces as a Salute to the Town. we were met by all the village and received a harty welcom from its inhabitiants."

Although it was Charbonneau who was on the payroll, his teenage wife, Sacagawea, proved to be very valuable in her contributions to the Corps of Discovery. She assisted in translating with the Indians, sewed clothing from hides to replace worn out clothing, made moccasins to replace worn out shoes, used her skills in medicine, and was invaluable in locating edible plants. She cared for Clark and others when they were ill. In return, Clark took care of Sacagawea during a ten-day illness that she experienced. Sacagawea's one request while at Fort Clatsop was to go down to the ocean and see it for herself, which she did. Lewis and Clark named a river after her for her quick work rescuing their books and documents when a canoe almost tipped over in the river.

By the end of the journey, one only team member had died. Sergeant Charles Floyd died in August 1804 from a medical emergency. After the expedition, Lewis was appointed Governor of the Louisiana Territory. Over the next few years, he suffered from depression. Lewis died in 1809 from a gunshot wound while traveling to visit President Jefferson. Whether he took his own life or was murdered has never been established. Clark was made a brigadier general of the Louisiana militia and an Indian agent for the Louisiana Territory. He later became governor of Missouri. He died in 1838 at the age of sixty-nine.

1

Only in Oregon

The Oregon Territory was established in 1848. At that time the Oregon Territory encompassed all of Oregon, Washington, Idaho, and a small portion of Wyoming and Montana. When Oregon became a state in 1859, the land was divided into what we know today.

Alis volat propiis.

The state of Oregon's motto is *Alis volat propiis.* The expression translates from Latin to English meaning, "She flies with her own wings." The motto was the first symbol adopted by the Oregon State Legislature in 1854.

William Harrison Boring was a pioneer who arrived in Oregon in 1856. He established the local post office, and in doing so, named the town Boring.

Boring, Oregon has a sister city: Dull, Scotland. In creating the sister city, the officials in Boring made a declaration stating their desire for “continued freedom, successful commerce, safety and prosperity for each community and its residents.”

The Oregon legislature signed into law that every August 9 would be Boring and Dull Day. Celebrations are held in each town.

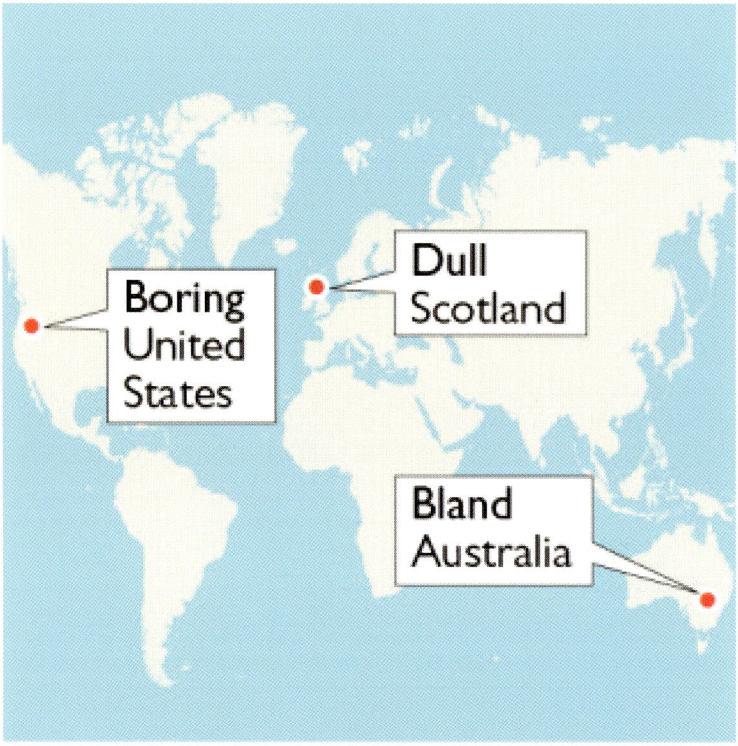

Left: When the town officials in Bland, Australia, heard about the sister cities of Boring and Dull, they joined in the fun.

Below: Bland, Australia's slogan is: Bland, far from Dull and Boring.

The Bigfoot trap located near the Applegate Lake is said to be the only one in the world. It was built in 1974 by the North American Wildlife Research Team. The trap was constructed of wooden slats, steel bolts, and plates. The trap measures ten feet long by ten feet wide. To date, there have been no sightings of the elusive Bigfoot, or Sasquatch, as he is sometimes called.

This “Octopus Tree” is located near Cape Meares Lighthouse. It is a Sitka Spruce that is shaped like an upside-down octopus. It is estimated to be 200-300 years old.

Rome, Oregon, was not built in a day. Rome got its start in 1909 when the town was established. It was named after the unique rock formations.

Legend of the Myrtle Tree

"Instead of the thorn shall come up the fir tree, and instead of the brier shall come up the Myrtle tree: and it shall be to the Lord for a name, for an everlasting sign that shall not be cut off." ISAIAH,55:13

America's most beautiful hardwood comes from the Myrtle tree. Rarest of all woods, the symmetrical, broadleaf, evergreen Myrtle grows only in Southwestern Oregon (Coos and Curry counties) and the Biblical lands of Palestine.

The coloring of the wood is unique, varying from a sedate, satiny gray to riotously, multicolored grains of red, yellow, and brown, with many burls and shapes in its grain. It takes a century or more for the Myrtle to grow to commercial size. Green unseasoned logs will not float.

There are very few places in the world where Myrtlewood trees grow. They are known to grow in Jerusalem, along the Oregon and California coasts, and in the Sierra foothills in California.

REDEEMABLE
JUNE 15, 1933
TO
JULY 15, 1933
CITY OF
NORTH BEND
OREGON
TREASURER
MAYOR

OREGON HISTORY
JEAN BAPTISTE CHARBONNEAU
1805-1866
THIS SITE MARKS THE FINAL RESTING PLACE
OF THE YOUNGEST MEMBER OF THE LEWIS AND
CLARK EXPEDITION, BORN TO SACAJAWEA AND
TOUSSAINT CHARBONNEAU AT FORT MANDAN
(NORTH DAKOTA) ON FEBRUARY 11, 1805.
BAPTISTE AND HIS MOTHER SYMBOLIZED THE
PEACEFUL NATURE OF THE "CORPS OF DIS-
COVERY". EDUCATED BY CAPTAIN WILLIAM
CLARK AT ST LOUIS, BAPTISTE AT AGE 18,
TRAVELED TO EUROPE WHERE HE SPENT SIX
YEARS, BECOMING FLUENT IN ENGLISH, GERMAN
FRENCH AND SPANISH. RETURNING TO AMERICA
IN 1829, HE RANGED THE FAR WEST FOR
NEARLY FOUR DECADES, AS MOUNTAIN MAN
GUIDE, INTERPRETER, MAGISTRATE AND FORTY
NINER. IN 1866, HE LEFT THE CALIFORNIA
GOLD FIELDS FOR A NEW STRIKE IN MONTANA,
CONTRACTED PNEUMONIA ENROUTE, REACHED
"INSKIP'S RANCHE", HERE, AND DIED ON MAY
16, 1866.

The Guinness World Records lists Portland's Mill Ends Park as the smallest park in the world. In 1948, newspaper columnist Dick Fagan got tired of looking at an empty spot where a light pole was supposed to be installed. Dick believed the space should be a park for leprechauns. The name "mill ends" comes from lumber mills where small pieces of wood can't be used due to their size.

Opposite above: They say that money doesn't grow on trees, but residents of North Bend, Oregon, may beg to differ. During the Great Depression, the only bank in town closed its doors. The North Bend City Council authorized $1,000 to be printed on discs of Myrtlewood and used to cover the city's payroll. When the local bank reopened, the city asked that people turn in their Myrtlewood money. Many chose to keep it as a souvenir.

Opposite below: There is a memorial for Sacajawea's son, Jean Baptiste Charbonneau, in Malheur County, as well as this sign. However, there is controversy as to where he is buried. Many believe he died in Malheur County after leaving Placer County, California, on his way home to the Wind River Indian Reservation in Wyoming. Others vehemently believe he died and was buried in Wyoming.

In 1960, Johnny Cash released his song, "Lumberjack," after spending time in Oregon. In the song he reminisces about his time working as a lumberjack. In part the lyrics are, "Ride this train to Roseburg, Oregon. Now there's a town for you. And you talk about rough. You know a lot of places in the country claim Paul Bunyon lived there. But you should have seen Roseburg when me and my daddy come there."

Oregon has one of four municipal elevators in the world. The others are in Brazil, Switzerland, and Sweden. The residences in Oregon City were built above the business area. Residents had to climb stairs until a municipal elevator was built in 1914. The original elevator was water powered until electricity was added in 1924. A new elevator was built in 1954.

In 1935, Angus Bowman requested permission from the Ashland City Council to produce three Shakespeare plays. They reluctantly agreed to two plays, as long as he promised to use the stage for boxing matches during the day. They reasoned that the income from the boxing matches would offset the financial loss from the plays. As it turned out, the plays offset the financial deficit from the boxing matches.

The Skiway Tram was constructed to connect Government Camp and Timberline Lodge. The tram was short lived but did operate in the 1950s. The tram buses were converted city buses. They were nicknamed "cloudliners," and "flying buses." The tram was held in the air by thirty-eight steel towers and twenty-five miles of 1.50-inch diameter cables. The cost to ride the tram was 75 cents one-way or $1.50 round trip.

Sitting at an elevation of 6,000 feet, the Timberline Lodge was extremely challenging to build in 1937. The 55,000 square foot lodge was built using native materials. The chimney contains 499 tons of stone and soars 92 feet in the air. The ironwork on the gates was made by hand using old railroad tracks. The solid fir beams in the lobby were shaped by hand using an ax.

During the night of August 6, 1959, a fire broke out in downtown Roseburg. A truck from Pacific Powder Company was parked downtown. The truck was loaded with four tons of solid ammonium nitrate fertilizer and two tons of dynamite. The truck caught fire and within minutes the explosion leveled downtown Roseburg.

Above: The explosion and fire became known as the "Roseburg Blast." Fourteen people died and more than a hundred were injured. The Roseburg Blast became the catalyst for identifying the chemicals being transported and placing safety protocols on the loads. It was also used to encourage cities and towns across America to be prepared for an emergency.

Left: The city of Portland would have been named Boston if a coin toss had gone differently. *The Herald and News* reported that two early settlers in Oregon—one from Boston Massachusetts, the other from Portland, Maine—flipped a coin to determine the name of their new town.

Eugene is known as Tracktown U.S.A. The Olympic trials have been held in Eugene and they have turned out many of their own Olympic champions. Additionally, the University of Oregon is well renowned for their track and field program.

The Tillamook State Forest suffered large scale fires during the Great Depression. After the fires were put out, workers were needed to go into the forests to salvage any usable wood. A logging camp was set up in the forest. Nearby residents began referring to the workers as idiots, due to the amount of work required. They also named a nearby creek Idiot Creek. There are no remaining residents.

In Oregon there is Zig Zag Mountain, Zig Zag Canyon, and Zig Zag River. In 1845, Joel Palmer wrote in his journal about descending the canyon and described having to zigzag a number of times. The town of Zig Zag was established in 1917. The following year the name was changed to ZigZag.

The expression, "Every Tom, Dick, and Harry," has been around for more than a century. In Oregon there is a mountain range called, "Tom, Dick, and Harry."

Sometimes it is easier to not have a name. The "No Name Lake" is pictured.

Oregon even has its own Christmas Valley. In the 1960s, developers built a lodge, three model homes, an artificial lake, an eight-unit motel, and an air field. Their company planes brought people from Southern California trying to entice them to buy plots of land starting at $59 an acre. A drive through Christmas Valley shows street signs such as Jingle Bell Road. In the end, it was not a successful project.

Oregon has a town called Sisters named after the nearby Three Sisters Mountains.

Above: The state also has a town called Brothers.

Right: Known as "Balancing Rocks," these formations are the result of geological activity. Natural erosion caused the rocks to appear to be balancing. The formations are believed to be at least 20,000 years old.

The Oregon Caves National Monument sits on 480 acres in Southern Oregon. It is known as "Oregon's Marble Halls" due to the limestone that metamorphosed into marble millions of years ago.

The Humongous Fungus, AKA the Honey Mushroom, is thought to be the largest living organism in the world based on mass, area, and volume. It resides in Harney County and is estimated to be at least 8,000 years old. It covers approximately 2,240 acres and weighs an estimated 35,000 tons.

The Dee Wright Observatory is pictured. At an elevation of 5,187 feet, it offers a view of Mount Washington and the Three Sisters Wilderness Area. It sits atop the lava flow that erupted from both the Yapoah Cone and an earlier flow from Little Belknap Crater. Both of these flows occurred more than 2,000 years ago.

Fort Rock is a tuff ring located on an Ice Age lakebed. It was originally an island. It measures approximately 4,460 feet in diameter and stands an estimated 200 feet tall. Fort Rock was created when basalt magma rose to the surface and encountered the bottom of the lake.

Thousands of years ago, a lake covered the Fort Rock Basin. The cave was created by winds that created enough erosion to make an indentation. Although the lake disappeared thousands of years ago, the cave remains.

These woven sagebrush sandals were located in the Fort Rock Cave. They are estimated to be more than 9,000 years old based on radiocarbon dating. The sandals are thought to be the oldest known footwear in the world. These sandals and others similar to them were located underneath volcanic ash that was determined to be from the eruption of Mount Mazama which occurred an estimated 7,700 years ago.

Right: Crater Lake National Park is the only National Park in Oregon. It was originally a volcano known as Mount Mazama. For more than half-a-million years, it had small eruptions that spewed pumice, ash and cinders. Over time magna vents and cones developed which weakened its structure. Approximately 7,700 years ago, the volcano had such a massive eruption that it could no longer support itself, and it collapsed.

Below: At first the caldera was too hot to hold water but eventually it did fill with snow and rainwater. At a depth of approximately 1,949 feet, Crater Lake is the deepest lake in the United States. Crater Lake became a national park in 1902.

Above: Known as the "Old Man of the Lake," this log has been floating vertically in Crater Lake for at least 125 years. It is thought to be a hemlock tree. The diameter measures approximately two feet and it rises about four feet above the water. The Old Man travels a great distance around the lake. [*Photo courtesy of Crater Lake National Park*]

Below left: This twenty-six-foot-tall statue was a "Big Friend" for a Texaco gas station in Aloha. Big Friend statues were placed at Texaco gas stations across the country. He was damaged in a storm and taken to Harvey's Marina to have his fiberglass repaired. No one ever came to pick him up, so Ed Harvey put a new head on him, and he became a giant rabbit, just like in the movie, *Harvey*.

Below right: Standing guard at twenty-nine feet tall, "the Bird," as he is known, has been welcoming customers to the Blackbird Store in Medford for decades. He has been known to sport a pair of shorts and a tank top during the warmer months and a Santa hat and candy cane during the month of December.

Above: Nessie has been greeting visitors to the Newport Aquarium Village for years. At twenty-five feet long, Nessie was created to resemble the Kronsaurus.

Right: The Paul Bunyon statue in Portland was built in 1959 to celebrate the state's centennial celebration. The statue, made of concrete and metal, stands thirty-one feet tall.

The Astoria column reaches 600 feet above sea level. The top can be reached by way of 164 steps. The Astoria column can be seen in the movies *The Goonies*, *Free Willy*, *Kindergarten Cop*, and *Teenage Mutant Ninja Turtles III*.

The Scappoose Peace Candle was created using 45,000 pounds of red candle wax to promote the Brock Candles Inc. factory. The candle was originally a silo. The wick was lit when it was first created in 1971 using a special sixty-foot-long match.

At seventy-two feet tall, this barber pole in Forest Grove is the tallest in the world. Forest Grove is known as "Ballard Town U.S.A." for their barbershop quartets. They have been winning competitions for decades.

The creator of The Enchanted Forest, Roger Tofte, and his family, opened to the public on August 8, 1971, after two years of building the Storybook Trail. Roger created The Enchanted Forest for families to enjoy. Over the years the Tofte family has added to The Enchanted Forest and now three generations of their family welcome guests for what they call, "something unique, with a lot of variety."

The Nelson family opened their Prehistoric Gardens in 1955 so that generations of families could enjoy the park that is occupied by dinosaurs and other prehistoric creatures. It took Mr. Nelson four years to construct the Brachiosaurs which stands forty-six feet tall and measures eighty-six feet in length. The Brachiosaurs is one of twenty-three dinosaurs at the park, each of which was built based on the size of their fossil skeleton.

Oregon is the only state in America that has a double-sided flag with two separate images.

Oregon was the thirty-third state admitted to the Union. For that reason, there are thirty-three stars on the flag.

The Oregon Legislature adopted the North American Beaver as the state animal in 1969. Early in Oregon's history, the beaver was hunted, almost to the point of extinction. Oncc controls were put in place, the beaver once again became a part of Oregon.

Oregon plays an important role in the Pacific Crest Trail. The entire trail spanning from the Mexican border to the Canadian border is 2,650 miles. Of those, 456 miles are in Oregon.

This vintage postcard shows what Fort Clatsop is believed to have looked like.

The Lewis and Clark expedition team was dependent on salt to preserve the meat from their hunting. This vintage postcard shows a replica of what their salt distilling stove and their five "kittles" might have looked like.

This twenty-six-foot canoe crafted of concrete stands in memory of Chief Comcomly. He was a friend to Lewis and Clark and their expedition team. He also helped John Jacob Astor's men establish their fort in what became known as Astoria.

Oregon is known for its timber. The men pictured are using a hand saw to chop down a gigantic tree.

Above: Pendleton Woolen Mill opened in 1909 and since then, they have been keeping Oregonians and people around the world warm. Their first blankets were designed for the nearby Nez Pierce Indians. Their popularity expanded to other Indian tribes throughout the Southwest. The blankets were used as ceremonial robes by the tribes. Six generations of the Bishop family have maintained a brand that is known for its quality and distinctive styling.

Left: The USS *Blueback* began its career in 1959 as the U.S. Navy's last diesel submarine. Its teardrop hull design made for faster speeds and greater maneuverability. In 1961, it traveled underwater from Yokosuka, Japan, to San Diego. The 5,340-mile journey was the longest-ever trip by a diesel submarine. Before it was decommissioned in 1990, it starred in the movie, *Hunt for Red October*. It arrived in Portland in 1994.

Oregon is home to the Spruce Goose, a gigantic wooden airplane. The airplane was constructed out of wood during World War II when metals were rationed. It was supposed to move troops and material during World War II, but it wasn't completed in time. It made one flight, albeit just one mile at an altitude of seventy feet. It was brought to the Evergreen Aviation and Space Museum in 1993.

The only house designed by Frank Lloyd Wright in Oregon is located in Silverton. It was designed in 1957 for Conrad and Evelyn Gordon. It was part of Wright's "Usonian" concept which created more modest Frank Lloyd Wright houses without sacrificing his vision of harmony between the house and its surroundings. It 2001, the house was dismantled and moved from a farm to the Oregon Garden where it was carefully reassembled.

Above: This meteorite was discovered in Willamette Valley in 1902. It is the largest meteorite in the United States and the sixth largest in the world. The Willamette Meteorite, as it is known, is made of iron-nickel and weighs 15.50 tons. The Clackamas Chinook Indians referred to it as *Tomanowos.* It resides at the American Museum of Natural History in New York City.

Left: The Pendleton Rodeo is well known throughout the United States. It began small in 1909 but has grown steadily every year.

It has been called a UFO, but it is actually a boat that was constructed in 1973. Richard Ensign spent two years and $10,000 building what he referred to as a "novel boat." It is thirty-one feet in circumference. There were living quarters for eight people. Richard told *The Capital Journal*, "It's designed to be an all-weather craft." The boat is located on Sauvie Island.

Interstate 5 runs from the Mexican border to the Canadian border. The Siskiyou Summit is located at the California-Oregon border. At an elevation of 4,310 feet, it is the highest elevation on Interstate 5.

45TH
PARALLEL
HALFWAY BETWEEN
THE EQUATOR AND
THE NORTH POLE

20 WEST
Newport, OR
3,365 MILES
ONE WAY

In Newport, a similar sign reads that it is 3,365 miles to Boston, Massachusetts. U.S. 20 is the longest continuous road in America, and it connects the two states.

Opposite above: The Earth's equator crosses North America, Europe, Asia, the Pacific Ocean, and the Atlantic Ocean. In Oregon, the 45th parallel begins at the coast and runs across the state just above Salem.

Opposite below: In Boston, Massachusetts, there is a road sign stating that it is 3,365 miles to Newport, Oregon.

During World War II, the Japanese sent thousands of balloon bombs over the Pacific Ocean with the intent that they would land on American soil and kill civilians. The balloon bombs were approximately seventy feet tall and thirty feet across. The covers were made from layers of paper. Inside was a metal ring holding the hydrogen filled bombs. Most of the balloon bombs sank in the Pacific Ocean.

Above: On May 5, 1945, Reverend Archie Mitchell, his wife, Elsie (who was pregnant with their first child), and five children from their church went on a picnic. While Archie was parking the car, the others discovered a balloon bomb. Within moments, it exploded, killing Elsie and the five children. The children who died ranged in age from eleven to fourteen.

Right: The deaths of Elsie and the children were the only casualties on the mainland United States during World War II as a result of enemy action. The area where the balloon bomb exploded was dedicated as the Mitchell Monument. A Ponderosa pine tree still bears shrapnel from the explosion.

Fort Stevens was built just before the Civil War ended. Its original purpose was to protect the Columbia River. During World War II, Fort Stevens was fired upon by the *I-25*, an enemy submarine. Fort Stevens did not fire back, as they believed the submarine was out of range. Prior to this, the last time the mainland United States had been shelled upon was during the War of 1812.

Camp Adair was a training facility for the United States Army during World War II. It was located near Corvallis. Camp Adair was named for Henry Rodney Adair, who was the first Oregonian to be killed in the 1916 Mexican Border Clash. The 91st Infantry, the 96th Infantry, the 70th Infantry, and the 104th Infantry trained at Camp Adair. Part of Camp Adair held Prisoners of War (POWs) during World War II.

Camp Adair also trained nurses prior to them being sent overseas. Due to training in harsh weather conditions, the facility took on the nickname of "Swamp Adair." After World War II, Camp Adair served as a military hospital for the United States Navy for a period of time.

Camp Abbott was a training facility for the U.S. Army Corps of Engineers. It opened during World War II outside of Bend. The site was on the Deschutes River and on a private ranch. The U.S. Army chose the area for its similarities to the terrain in Europe where the troops would be fighting. It was the only training facility for the western states. The other two training facilities were in Virginia and Missouri.

Camp Abbott closed soon after World War II ended. Most of the camp was razed and the land returned to its original use. All that remains today of Camp Abbott is a building that was used for their training, and for a time, their officer's club. Today that building is part of the Sunriver Resort as pictured.

Camp White in Jackson County was a military cantonment during World War II. More than 40,000 soldiers trained at Camp White before being sent overseas. Camp White was home to the 91st Division which was designated as a triangular division, meaning that the infantry, artillery, medical staff, and engineers were all under one commander. [*Eagle Point Historical Society*]

Nurses also trained at Camp White prior to going overseas. In 1942, the U.S. Government began detaining Germans as Prisoners of War (POWs.) A total of 1,600 Germans were held at Camp White. In 1943, the government decided that the POWs could work in industries that did not compete with American workers. Many of the POWs worked in the local orchards for 80 cents per day. [*Eagle Point Historical Society*]

During World War II, the U.S. Forest Service heard a plane overhead near Brookings. It flew a short distance into the forest, then retreated quickly. A Forest Service employee fired at the plane with unknown results. Soon after, a fire was detected near Mount Emily. The plane had come off a Japanese submarine located offshore and dropped an incendiary bomb. The fire was put out and there were no injuries.

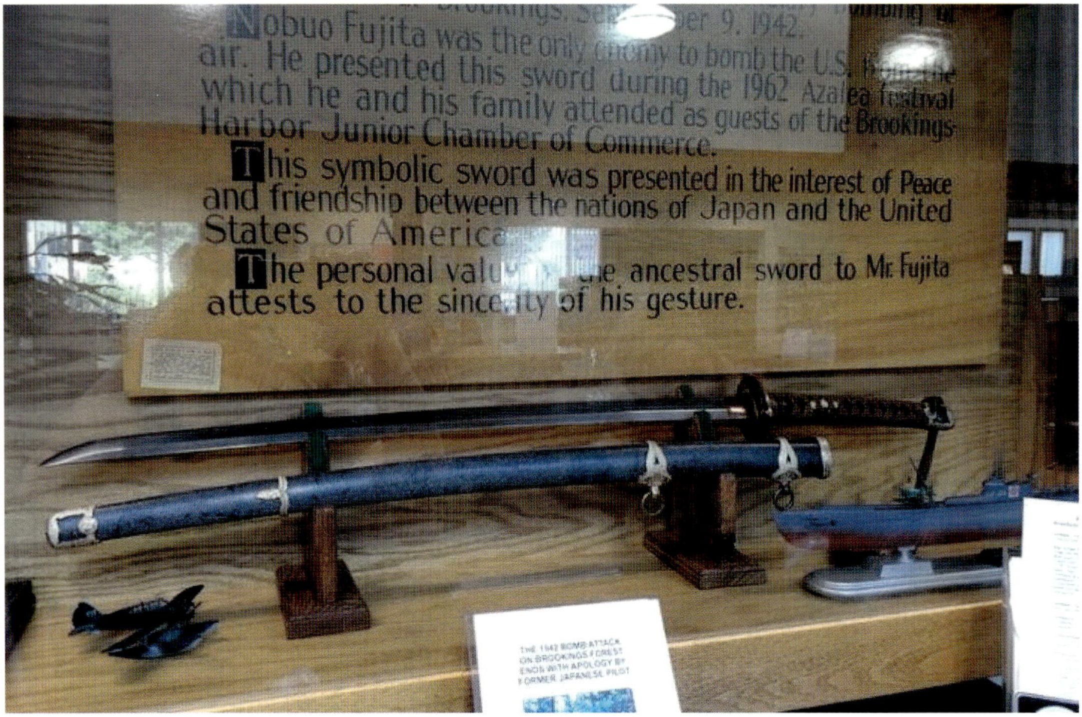

Twenty years later, the pilot of that plane, Nubuo Fujita, returned to Brookings through an international goodwill project. He presented a 500-year-old Samurai sword to the City of Brookings as a gesture of goodwill and peace between the two nations.

When driving past Silent Mountain, it is expected that there will be complete silence in the car. No one is supposed to talk, no music is to be played, and the radio should be turned off.

The Smith Rock State Park stretches for more than 600 acres in Central Oregon. This geological wonderland shoots 600 feet above the river. The spires, cliffs, and canyonlands were formed through volcanic eruptions more than twenty-seven million years ago.

The original Crooked River was obliterated by lava flows millions of years ago. The river seen today is a result of water building up from the Blue Mountains and then overflowing across the lava.

Hells Canyon is the deepest river gorge in North America. At 7,993 feet deep, it even surpasses the Grand Canyon. Hells Canyon borders Oregon, Washington, and Idaho.

The Owyhee River was named by explorer Peter Skeen Ogden to honor the Hawaiians who disappeared while exploring the river in 1818. The word *Owyhee* was the phonetic spelling for "Hawaii." The remoteness of the region has meant that it has remained virtually untouched in some parts.

Not to be out down by Yellowstone National Park, Oregon has its own geyser. It is located at Geyser Hunters Hot Springs.

The first chair lift at Mount Hood was built in 1933. It was another forty years before a chair life was installed on the upper slopes. The upper chair lift replaced the snowcat that had been used to take people to the top so they could ski down.

Multnomah Falls drops more than 600 feet and is the tallest waterfall in Oregon. As far back as 1884, the railroad brought tourists to see the two-tiered waterfall. Tourism increased exponentially when automobiles and paved roads were introduced.

The Painted Hills date back millions of years ago when the area was an ancient river floodplain. The varying shades came about as the climate changed. The Painted Hills span more than 3,000 acres in Wheeler County.

2

Made in Oregon

Oregon offers locals and visitors everything from snow-capped mountains and sage covered lava beds to ocean waves and painted hills. Oregon's scenic beauty has brought movie productions teams to Oregon to film. A few of the movies made in Oregon are included here. Also included are some of the items that put Oregon on the map.

The tater tot could be considered one of the best examples of upcycling. The Ore-Ida company, (short for Oregon-Idaho) began making tater tots in 1953. Up to that time they had been making French fries, but they noticed a large portion of the potatoes were going to waste. Instead of throwing away the excess, they made the bits into what became known as tater tots.

When pioneer Seth Lewelling left Iowa, he packed fruit trees in sand and planted them once he arrived in Oregon. He established a large variety of fruit orchards. Seth is credited with introducing Bing Cherries to the world. One of the first cherries was named Lewelling; the other he named for the foreman on his ranch, Ah Bing. An elementary school in Milwaukie is named for Seth.

Above left: The maraschino cherry was popular in Europe for centuries, but the cherries grown in America were not adapting to the preservation method. In the 1920s, a professor at Oregon State University, Ernest Wiegand, was asked to create a solution so that the cherries grown in the United States could be preserved. After experimenting for six years, he created a brine solution that is still in use today.

Above right: Oregon has the Marionberry to its credit. It was developed at Oregon State University by George Waldo in the 1940s. It is a cross between the Chehalem berry and the Olallie berry. It is named after Marion County.

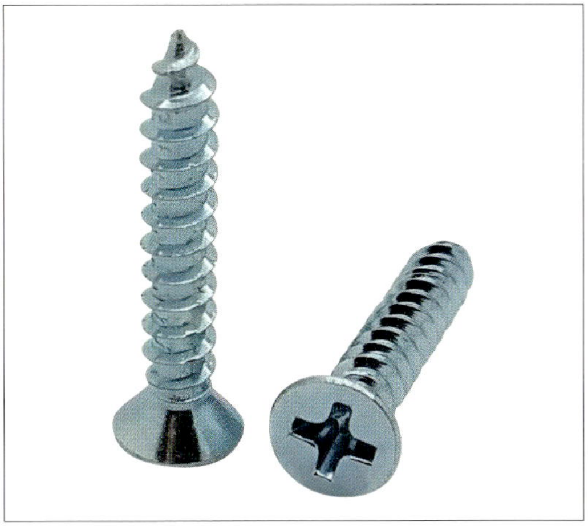

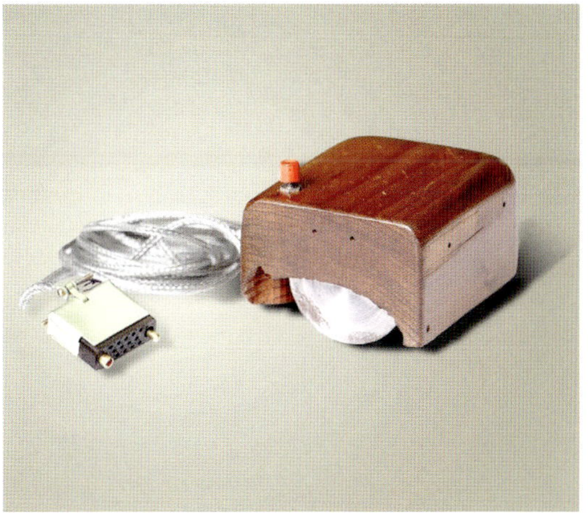

Above left: It was John P. Thompson of Portland who developed the screw and screwdriver known today as the Phillips. When he was not able to market the products, he sold the items and the patents to Henry Frank Phillips, also of Oregon. Henry created the Phillips Screw Company and made the products a household name.

Above right: Douglas Carl Engelbart of Oregon was the co-founder of the computer mouse. Douglas had the vision for a device with two wheels; one to move vertically, the other to move horizontally. He teamed up with Bill English and they developed a prototype. In 1970, they received a patent. They named it a mouse because they thought the cord that came out of the wooden box looked like the tail of a mouse.

Alfred Carlton Gilbert was born in Salem in 1884. He attended the Tualatin Academy and Pacific University before transferring to Yale. He became an Olympic athlete and later a successful inventor. He received more than 150 patents for his inventions. Although he did not invent the American Flyer toy train, he bought the existing company and made improvements to the trains so they appeared more realistic.

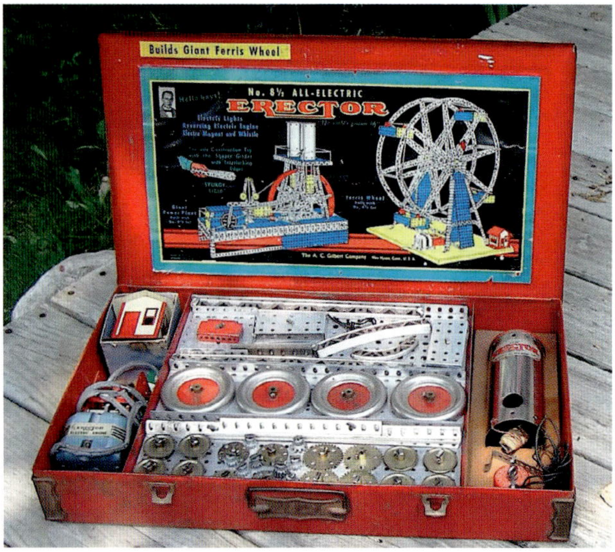

Above left: While working in New York, Alfred Gilbert watched heavy construction taking place on the railroad. Alfred envisioned a toy that would allow people to construct the same type of projects. In 1913, he introduced the Erector Set. During World War I, the Council of National Defense proposed a ban on toys. Alfred fought against the idea and ultimately won. This earned him the name of, "The man who saved Christmas."

Above right: Also known as filberts, the hazelnut crop is very important to Oregon's agriculture industry. Sam Strickland is credited with planting the first hazelnut tree in 1858 in Scottsburg.

Portland is known as the "City of Roses." The Portland International Rose Test Garden is pictured. In began in 1918, making it the oldest continuously operating public rose test garden in the United States. It is home to more than 10,000 roses.

In 1985, the Iverson family invited the locals to view their tulip farm over Easter weekend. Since then, the Wooden Shoe Tulip Farm has grown to forty acres and has been visited by people from every state in America and from 140 countries. Every year from March to May, they open their farm so that people can enjoy tulips as far as the eye can see.

The Schloe family has been welcoming visitors to their Swan Island Dahlia Farm in Canby for generations. Their forty-acre dahlia farm is the largest in the United States. Visitors can enjoy hundreds of varieties of the beautiful flowers.

Since 1946, the Schreiner family has been growing all types of varieties of bearded irises at their family farm in Salem. The family welcomes visitors every year to enjoy their award-winning bearded irises planted on over 100 acres.

Charles McFarlin is credited with planting the first crop of cranberries in Bandon in 1885. He planted five acres with a wild variety that he brought from Massachusetts. Today, Bandon is known as the "Cranberry Capital of Oregon." Cranberries are grown in other parts of the world, but the United States is the leader. The cranberries grown in Oregon have a longer growing season, which results in a deeper color.

Above: Brookings is well known for Easter lilies. This began when Louis Houghton arrived in town with a suitcase of hybrid lily bulbs. He had recently retired from the U.S. Department of Agriculture and believed the lilies would grow well in Brookings. He gave away the bulbs to anyone interested in planting them. There wasn't much interest in the beginning, but over the years the crops gained in popularity.

Right: Oregon is the grass seed capital of the world. Most of the grass seed is produced in the Willamette Valley, which has the perfect climate for grass seed.

Above: The most important part of the movie *Free Willy* was filmed in Hammond. Willy jumped for his freedom from the breakwater at the Hammond Marina. The star of the movie, Keiko, lived at the Oregon Coast Aquarium in Newport for three years before returning to his homeland of Iceland.

Below: It is not every movie that has such a strong following that decades later, an entire day is devoted to celebrate the movie, but that is the case with *The Goonies*. The movie was filmed primarily in Astoria. Decades later, the town celebrates Goonies Day with fun activities.

Another Oregon movie with a cult following is *Animal House*. The movie was partially filmed in and around Eugene in 1977. The University of Oregon received $20,000 for allowing the film company to use the campus for filming. Their only stipulation was that the name of the university not be identified in the film. Half a century later, the university is well known as the home of this fan favorite.

The movie *One Flew Over the Cuckoo's Nest* was partially filmed in and around Salem and on the Oregon coast in 1975. The Oregon State Hospital was used for the hospital scenes. The movie was adapted from the novel written by Ken Kesey. The novel and the movie take place in a psychiatric hospital. The movie went onto great acclaim, winning many awards.

Astoria was home to the movie *Kindergarten Cop*. The film crew arrived in 1990 and began filming at the Astor Elementary School. They also filmed in downtown Astoria and along the Oregon coast.

In the movie *Stand By Me*, the fictional town of Castle Rock, Oregon, was actually filmed in Brownsville, Cottage Grove, Eugene, Franklin, Veneta, and Junction City. The movie was filmed in 1986 and is more popular today than when it was released.

3

The Oregon Coast

For hundreds of years, ships traveled around the globe to trade goods with the Indians along the Oregon coast. With ships came shipwrecks, and Oregon has had more than its fair share of shipwrecks. The lack of lighthouses, coupled with heavy fog and gale force winds, proved to be too much for many vessels.

Bayocean was a land development that advertised, "The environments of Bayocean, natural and social, are unequal; it logically becomes the natural selection for those seeking health, for those desirous of pleasure and society; as an investment, its advantages are apparent to the layman as well as the engineer and capitalist." At the heart of the development was the Bayocean Natatorium that covered an entire block as pictured.

The Oregon coast is home to many seals and sea lions. The Pacific harbor seal, the northern fur seal, the northern elephant seal, the California sea lion, and the Steller sea lion all make their home along the Oregon coast.

Opposite above: By the late 1920s, it became apparent that the town of Bayocean was slowing slipping into the ocean. The hotel was the first to slip into the ocean, followed by the natatorium. Many of the homes and businesses were far enough back that they were able to survive for years, but their foundations were cracking and tilting.

Opposite below: The original promotional materials boasted of Bayocean being so close to the Pacific Ocean. That proved to be its downfall as the buildings fell one by one into the Pacific Ocean. The last house slipped into the deep waters in 1960. Today, nothing remains of the resort town.

Oregon is known for its forests, and for its ocean, but this forest is actually in the ocean. The Neskowin Ghost Forest is believed to be more than 2,000 years old. The tree stumps are the remains of a Sitka spruce forest that was likely destroyed in an earthquake, then covered with mud from landslides or a tsunami. The trees were 150 feet tall and 200 years old when they were buried.

John Jacob Astor was a fur trader in New York when he learned about the furs on the west coast. He formed the Pacific Fur Company. He sent one expedition overland led by William Price Hunt. He sent another team on his ship the *Tonquin*. The teams set up a trading post and named it Fort Astoria in 1811. A replica of the fort is pictured in this vintage postcard.

Looking at Thor's Well, it appears that the ocean water is going down a huge drain. Thor's Well is actually a hole in a rock that is approximately twenty feet deep. At high tide, the water can gush back out and put on a show. It is located near Cape Perpetua.

Haystack Rock at Cannon Beach soars 235 feet in the air. It was created from lava flows from the Blue Mountains and the Columbia River between fifteen and seventeen million years ago.

Above: The Devil's Punchbowl is located near Otter Crest. When ocean water enters the Devil's Punchbowl, it is violently tossed and churned before exiting.

Left: Arch Rock is a natural formation at Harris Beach. Thousands of years of erosion caused the hole to form in the arch.

This three-masted ship from Great Britain wrecked near Manzanita on October 1, 1913. The *Glenesslin* was enroute to the Columbia River, having left Brazil on May 28, 1913. The ship was supposed to pick up a load of wheat and return to Great Britain, as she had done in the past. The crew of twenty-one were rescued. Paul Bartels is using an early-day camera to take a photograph.

The *Santa Clara* wrecked on November 2, 1915. The 233-foot-long vessel was on its way to San Francisco from Portland. In addition to freight, there were forty-eight passengers. Lifeboats were launched at Marshfield and twenty-nine people were saved.

The S.S. *Bandon* wrecked at Port Orford on August 27, 1916. The ship was owned by A. F. Estabrook. It was the second ship of his to wreck in under one year. The Marine Underwriters spent a month trying to float the ship off the rocks. They finally had to give up and sell the wreckage for $1,500.

When the *Laurel* crashed on the rocks of Peacock Spit, the Coast Guard had to make two trips to the wreckage to collect all thirty-two members of the crew. There were no passengers on board. Captain Louis Johnson initially refused any attempts to be rescued. He stayed with the ship for three nights huddled in the radio cabin. He was found negligent for the crash and suspended for ninety days.

On March 2, 1929, the *Sujameco* went aground near Coos Bay. A month later, J. O. Fisher, W. E. Swan, Ernest Peterson, and Milo Pierson drove a Dodge automobile up to the shipwreck. To get there, they had to cross an old bridge, endure mud holes, sinking sand, dodge tree stumps and saw logs, and avoid quicksand. For the last part, Milo's team of horses helped pull the car through the sand.

The mysterious *George L. Olson* shipwreck is shown. Shifting winds and changing tides revealed the hulk of this steam schooner that was used to haul lumber. It was discovered in 2008 after being buried for almost seventy years. A large portion of the shipwreck has since disappeared.

The *Admiral Benson* was a coastal liner of the Pacific Steamship Company. It ran aground on February 15, 1930. Mrs. J. W. Weinrabe told reporters that the ship's officers dispelled the passenger's fears, assuring them that everything was fine. She described the dining room being full of music, dancers, and balloons, when she saw people falling to the ground. The officers simply shouted, "On with the dances!"

The British ship, *Peter Iredale,* wrecked early on the morning of October 25, 1906. She had left Mexico twenty-nine days prior heading to pick up a load of wheat in Astoria and another load in Portland before returning home to Liverpool, England. It was Captain Lawrence's fifteenth time making the journey. He was exonerated from any negligence and the cause of the wreck was blamed on heavy fog and high winds.

Newspapers across the country reported, "The crew of the *Iredale* was in danger only during the few moments the masts, spars, and rigging were falling. The Iredale ran up the shelving sands with but little violence, and as soon as Captain Lawrence saw that grounding was inevitable, he summoned all hands aft and prepared to abandon the ship." Three weeks later the *Galena* ship went aground a few miles away.

The wreck of the *Peter Iredale* has been a popular tourist attraction. It is one of the few shipwrecks that is visible in the graveyard of the Pacific Ocean. In its prime it weighed 1,994 tons. It measured 287 feet long, forty feet across and twenty-three feet deep.

Above: The Cape Arago Lighthouse began illuminating the waters in 1866. By 1909, the breakers had worn a hole through the rock that the lighthouse sat on. A new lighthouse was built further back from the breakers. Cape Arago was named for the passenger boat, *Arago,* that crashed nearby. Fourteen people died in the wreck.

Left: During World War II, a Japanese airplane dropped incendiaries on Cape Blanco. Flames were seen and explosions were heard, but the investigators were not able to locate the incendiaries. A heavy smoke hung in the air. The land surrounding the lighthouse was too damp for a fire to start. Months later, the SS *Fort Comsum* was torpedoed off of Cape Blanco. The following day the radio station at Vancouver Island was shelled.

Cape Blanco and Heceta Head Lighthouse were built at the same time using the same building plans. They are frequently referred to as "the twins."

Left: The original Umpqua Lighthouse was lit for the first time in 1857. That lighthouse gave way in the 1860s after many storms. The replacement lighthouse was lit for the first time in 1894.

Below: The Cape Meares Lighthouse stands 217 feet above the ocean. The light was manufactured in Paris, France, in 1877. It arrived by ship on the Oregon coast and was packed by mules up to the cape. It lit up the coast for the first time in 1890. A celebration was held with people traveling by stagecoach, horse, muleback, and on foot. Bricks from the base were made from nearby clay.

The only way to get supplies and people to Tillamook Rock was in boatswain's chairs and cargo nets suspended from a large derrick boom.

While building the lighthouse, the construction crew lived in a leaky sixteen-foot-long shelter. For two weeks, hurricane-force winds pounded the shelter. By the time the skies cleared, they were drenched and hungry. The ocean was still raging so boats could not get close enough to send supplies. An officer constructed a kite and was able to fly dry clothing and food to the construction crew using the kite.

The Yaquina Bay Lighthouse was first lit in 1871. It was the only lighthouse built in Oregon that had the living quarters in the same building as the light. It was home to the United States Army Corps of Engineers from 1888-1896 while they built the north and south jetties at the mouth of Yaquina Bay. The U.S. Coast Guard used the lighthouse for their headquarters from 1906-1915.

Lightships served in areas where a lighthouse could not be built. The first lightship at the Columbia River was the *LV-50* which began operating in 1892. Over the years, other lightships replaced the original. Pictured is the *Columbia River Lightship*, also known as *WLV-604*. This vessel served from 1951-1979. The crew aboard had to be self-sufficient for periods of time when the waters prevented boats from bringing in supplies.